Hamilton Trivia Book

By Veronica Blue

Dear customer, we hope this book will bring you interesting times. If you have any suggestions for our next projects, do not hesitate to keep us informed. Thank you for your patronage.

Introduction

Hamilton: An American Musical is undoubtedly an amazing sung-and-rapped-through musical by Lin-Manuel Miranda. It tells the story of American Founding Father Alexander Hamilton. The show draws heavily from hip hop, as well as R&B, pop, soul, and traditional-style show tunes. It casts non-white actors as the Founding Fathers and other historical figures.

From its opening, Hamilton received critical acclaim. It premiered Off-Broadway on February 17th, 2015, with Miranda playing the role of Alexander Hamilton, where its several-month engagement was sold out. At the 70th Tony Awards, Hamilton received a record-breaking 16 nominations and won 11 awards, including Best Musical. It received the 2016 Pulitzer Prize for Drama.

No one could have predicted that a hip-hop-infused musical based on the life of Alexander Hamilton would become Broadway's hottest ticket, but that's exactly what happened when Lin-Manuel Miranda's Hamilton debuted in July 2015. A movie version of the show, recorded with the original cast and titled Hamilton: An American Musical, hit Disney Plus on July 3rd, 2015. Here is a book that contains some fun facts as well as memories about a legendary American Musical.

Contents

A. FACTS

23 Things You Might Not Have Known About Hamilton

1. Hamilton was inspired by Ron Chernow's biography of Alexander Hamilton.

Not long after his show In the Heights won four Tony Awards in 2008, Lin-Manuel Miranda went on vacation. Before he left, he picked up a biography called Alexander Hamilton. "I was just browsing the biography section. It could have been Truman," he told 60 Minutes. "I got to the part where a hurricane destroys St. Croix, where Hamilton is living. And he writes a poem about the carnage and this poem gets him off the island."

"That is part and parcel with the hip-hop narrative: writing your way out of your circumstances, writing the future you want to see for yourself," Miranda told The New York Times. "This is a guy who wrote at 14, 'I wish there was a war.' It doesn't get more hip-hop than that."

Miranda recalled to Vogue that "I Googled 'Alexander Hamilton hip-hop musical' and totally expected to see that someone had already written it. But no. So I got to work."

2. It took Miranda a year to write Hamilton's first song—and another year to write the second song.

He performed the song, "Alexander Hamilton," at the White House in 2009. "From what I hear," Questlove, who produced· the cast album, told Billboard, "the president won't cease to let you know that: 'The White House is where it began.'"

It took Miranda another year to craft Hamilton's anthem, "My Shot." "Every couplet needed to be the best couplet I ever wrote," Miranda told 60 Minutes. "That's how seriously I was taking it."

3. Miranda wrote Hamilton's lyrics on the move.

When Miranda needed to come up with the song lyrics, he told Smithsonian, he walked. "For Hamilton what I'd do is write at the piano until I had something I liked," he said. "I'd make a loop of it and put it in my headphones and then walk around until I had the lyrics. That's where the notebooks come in, sort of write what comes to me, bring it back to the piano. I kind of need to be ambulatory to write lyrics."

4. Hamilton started as a mixtape, not a musical.

Initially, Miranda said he was working on a concept album inspired by the life of Alexander Hamilton called The Hamilton Mixtape. "I always had an eye toward the stage for the story of Hamilton's life, but I began with the idea of a concept album, the way Andrew Lloyd Webber's Evita and Jesus Christ Superstar were albums before they were musicals," Miranda recounted to the Hollywood Reporter. "And I built this score by dream casting my favorite artists. I always imagined George Washington as a mix between Common and John Legend (a pretty good description of Christopher Jackson, actually, who plays our first president); Hercules Mulligan was Busta Rhymes; and Hamilton was modeled after my favorite polysyllabic rhyming heroes, Rakim, Big Pun, and Eminem."

The reason, he told The New York Times, was because "I wanted to be a little more selfish with this—I wanted the lyrics to have the density that my favorite hip-hop albums have … It was easier to think of it as a hip-hop album, because then I could really just pack the lyrics. [But] I only know how to write musicals." He performed 12 musical numbers from The Hamilton Mixtape at Lincoln Center's American Songbook series in January 2012; he began workshopping the show in 2014. It played The Public beginning in January 2015 and made the jump to Broadway in July 2015 (it officially opened in August).

5. Miranda did his research—both historically and musically—to write Hamilton.

In addition to reading Chernow's biography of Hamilton, Miranda read Hamilton's letters and works and visited sites important to the American Revolution in New York City. He explained to The Atlantic that, to understand Burr, he read The Heartbreak of Aaron Burr by H.W. Brands, and to nail the dueling code of the day, he picked up Affairs of Honor by Joanne Freeman. He wrote, for a time, at the Morris-Jumel Mansion, which Washington once used as a headquarters during the Revolutionary War. In October 2014, before the show began playing at The Public, he and director Thomas Kail went to the Weehawken, New Jersey, dueling ground where Burr shot Hamilton (the actual dueling grounds are covered by train tracks now, but there is a small memorial there).

Miranda also looked at other musicals before diving into Hamilton, like Jesus Christ Superstar and Les Miserables. "I really got my Les Miz on in this score, like being really smart about where to reintroduce a theme," he told The New Yorker. "In terms of how it accesses your tear ducts, nothing does it better than that show."

6. Ron chernow was a historical consultant for Hamilton.

Miranda met Chernow before he performed the song that would become "Alexander Hamilton" at the White House (in fact, he sang the song to Chernow in the biographer's living room), and soon Chernow became a consultant on the show. "[Miranda] was smart enough to know that the best way to dramatize this story was to stick as close to the facts as possible," Chernow told 60 Minutes.

"I'm theater people, and theater people, the only history they know is the history they know from other plays and musicals," Miranda told The Atlantic. "So to that end, I felt an enormous responsibility to be as historically accurate as possible, while still telling the most dramatic story possible. And that's why Ron Chernow is a historical consultant on the thing, and, you know, he was always sort of keeping us honest. And when I did part from the historical record or take dramatic license, I made sure I was able to defend it to Ron, because I knew that I was going to have to defend it in the real world. None of those choices are made lightly."

According to Smithsonian, Chernow looked at every draft and every song and assessed everything for accuracy.

7. Hamilton wasn't always sung through.

Hamilton is sung and rapped from start to finish, but it wasn't always that way. "We actually went down the road with a playwright," Miranda told Grantland. "There's a version of Act 1 where we had songs and they were the songs that are in the show, but we found that if you start with our opening number, you can't go back to speech. The ball is just thrown too high in the air."

8. One scene from Hamilton didn't make it onto the soundtrack.

The show features one scene that isn't sung, and which Miranda kept off of the cast album: In "Tomorrow There'll Be More of Us," which takes place between "Dear Theodosia" and "Non-Stop," Hamilton finds out that his friend Laurens has been killed. "I made a decision not to record this scene on the album, for two reasons," Miranda wrote on Tumblr:

"1) It really is more of a scene than a song, the only SCENE in our show, and I think its impact is at its fullest in production form. 2) As someone who grew up ONLY listening to cast albums (we ain't have money for a lot of Broadway shows, like most people) those withheld moments were REVELATIONS to me when I finally experienced them onstage, years later. Hamilton is sung through, and I wanted to have at least ONE revelation in store for you. I stand by the decision, and I think the album is better for it."

9. Miranda wrote King George's song in Hamilton, "you'll be back," on his honeymoon.

Because he's an interloper on the proceedings of Hamilton, King George's song, "You'll Be Back," is quite different from the rest of the show's numbers. "It's a throwback to a sixties Beatles tune," Jonathan Groff, who plays King George, told Vogue. "And it's a breakup song between America and England, which is fabulous. He's like, 'You're leaving me? Oh, really? Well, good luck with that.'" Miranda wrote the song while on his honeymoon in 2010 "without a piano around," he told Grantland.

10. The original version of the Hamilton song "My Shot" had an extra verse for Hercules Mulligan.

"I'm Hercules Mulligan, a tailor spying on the British Government / I take the measurements, information and then I smuggle it / Up to my brother's revolutionary covenant / I'm running with the Sons of Liberty, and I'm loving it," Mulligan raps. At that point, neither the Marquis de Lafayette nor John Laurens were part of the song. You can hear the rest of the demo here; portions of Mulligan's verse ended up in "Yorktown (World Turned Upside Down)."

11. Miranda wrote "Wait For It" on the subway.

"I was going to a friend's birthday party in [Brooklyn]," he said, when a lyric from the chorus to Aaron Burr's song, "Wait for It," came to him. "I sang the melody into the iPhone, then I went to the guy's party for 15 minutes, and wrote the rest of the song on the train back home."

12. The rap in "Guns And Ships" is really, really fast.

"I believe that form [rap] is uniquely suited to tell Hamilton's story, because it has more words per measure than any other musical genre," Miranda told 60 Minutes. "It has rhythm, and it has density, and if Hamilton had anything in his writing, it was this density." The use of rap helps Miranda pack more than 20,000 words into two and a half hours—roughly 144 words per minute, according to Leah Libresco at

FiveThirtyEight. "If Hamilton were sung at the pace of the other Broadway shows I looked at, it would take four to six hours," Libresco wrote. She found that the musical's fastest paced verse, from the song "Guns and Ships," clocked in at 6.3 words per second.

13. Hamilton's songs sample rap music and reference rap songs—as well as other musicals.

As a show that has its roots in rap, it's not surprising that Miranda has peppered Hamilton with rap references and samples: "My Shot" has elements of Mobb Deep's "Shook Ones Part II" and an homage to Notorious B.I.G.'s "Going Back to Cali"; the song "Ten Duel Commandments" samples B.I.G.'s "Ten Crack Commandments"; the opening to "Cabinet Battle #1" references Jay-Z's "Izzo (H.O.V.A.)" and contains parts of "The Message" by Grandmaster Flash; "Meet Me Inside" contains elements of DMX's "Party Up in Here (Up in Here)"; and "Cabinet Battle #2" references B.I.G's "Juicy (It's All Good)." These themes—and samples—show up in other songs throughout Hamilton.

Miranda pays homage to Broadway shows, too: He snatched a line from South Pacific for Burr ("I'm with you but the situation is fraught / You've got to be carefully taught," in

"My Shot"), makes reference to the song "Modern Major General" from Pirates of Penzance (when Washington sings, "I'm the model of a modern major general / the venerated Virginian veteran whose men are all / Lining up, to put me on a pedestal," in "Right Hand Man"), and put parts of "Nobody Needs to Know" from The Last Five Years in "Say No to This."

Miranda's lyrics are also packed with historical references. We decoded a few here, and many are annotating the lyrics on Genius (Miranda himself has also weighed in there). Miranda also wrote his own book of annotated lyrics, which he tweeted are "Not what you'd find on Genius, just things in my brain & heart."

14. At first, Miranda couldn't decide if he wanted to play Hamilton or Burr.

"I feel an equal affinity with Burr," he told The New Yorker. "Burr is every bit as smart as Hamilton, and every bit as gifted, and he comes from the same amount of loss as Hamilton. But because of the way they are wired Burr hangs back where Hamilton charges forward. I feel like I have been Burr in my life as many times as I have been Hamilton." But eventually, he chose Hamilton: "When I get called in for stuff for Hollywood, I get to be the best friend of the Caucasian lead.

If I want to play the main guy, I have found, I have to write it ... [As Hamilton], I get to be cockier than I really am; I get to be smarter than I really am; I get to be more impulsive than I really am—it's taking the reins off your id for two and a half hours."

Burr was played by Leslie Odom Jr. "I stupidly gave him a lot of the best songs," Miranda told Grantland. "'Wait for It' and 'The Room Where It Happens' are two of the best songs I've ever written in my life and he got them both."

15. Casting people of color in Hamilton's main roles was a deliberate choice.

"Our goal was: This is a story about America then, told by America now, and we want to eliminate any distance—our story should look the way our country looks," Miranda told The New York Times. "Then we found the best people to embody these parts. I think it's a very powerful statement without having to be a statement." The only main character played by a white actor is King George.

"When I think about what it would mean to me as a 13-, 14-year-old kid, to get this album or see this show—it can make me very emotional," Odom told The New York Times.

Later, Hamilton's producers would say that, "It is essential to the storytelling of Hamilton that the principal roles, which were written for nonwhite characters (excepting King George), be performed by nonwhite actors."

16. One of the most important characters in Hamilton is "the bullet."

One of the first characters to die in the show is a spy, who, after the song "You'll Be Back," is discovered by a British soldier who breaks her neck. The spy is played by Ariana DeBose, and after her on-stage execution, she becomes a character known as The Bullet—who is essentially death personified. As PopSugar notes, The Bullet foreshadows many of the show's deaths: In "Yorktown," she shakes hands with John Laurens, who dies not long after; in "Blow Us All Away," she flirts with Philip Hamilton, who later dies in a duel with George Eacker. And before she delivers the round that fatally wounds Hamilton in "The World Was Wide Enough," she has several interactions with the title character.

17. Hamilton's set is symbolic.

Hamilton set designer David Korins told the Washington Post that when designing the set, he decided on something that looked like an unfinished, mid-construction colonial-era building. "This is the story of the people who built the scaffolding upon which the country was built, so you see wooden period scaffolding up around a half-made wall to show a kind of aspirational space," he said. The turntables in the stage, meanwhile, were, according to the Post, "inspired by the whirlwind of history that sweeps up Hamilton, as well as the literal hurricane that hits the Caribbean island where he was born."

The set changes between acts—the brick walls (which are actually made of plastic and wood) behind the scaffolding get 8 feet taller, "because the country is progressing and that foundation is getting bigger," Korins told WaPo. Quills and parchment replace the rifles hanging on the walls, "because the war is over and now it's time to govern."

18. Running up and down the stairs of the Hamilton set can be exhausting.

When James Monroe Iglehart—who had previously played the Genie in Broadway's Aladdin—stepped into the roles of

Lafayette and Jefferson in Hamilton in 2017, he told Mental Floss that the toughest part of the show wasn't necessarily what one would expect. "The French accent is not the hardest, it's not the speed of the lyrics, it's not the show—it is the stairs," he said. "There are stairs going up, and then there are stairs going down. And there's stairs going down onstage, stairs going off. What you don't see are the two sets of stairs behind. So my first act as Marquis de Lafayette, I walk up the steps, I walk down the back steps, I dip the jacket, walk back on, walk up the steps again, walk down the steps. There's one song where I walk up the steps four times. Between 'Helpless' and 'Satisfied' I walk up the steps six times, because we have to rewind. My calves were like, 'What are you doing?' I mean, I did a cartwheel eight times a week and tap danced in Aladdin. But on this show, I cussed—I was like, 'What's up with this Stairmaster show you guys built?'"

19. The stars of Hamilton helped raise money for the orphanage Eliza Hamilton started.

In 1806, Eliza Hamilton was one of the founders of New York City's first private orphanage; these days, it's called Graham Windham. Miranda and Philippa Soo, who played Eliza in Hamilton, performed at an event to raise money for the organization. "What a time at the Graham

Windham luncheon today," he tweeted. "When the kids (from ELIZA'S ORGANIZATION) sang 'Eliza, you have done enough.' I mean..."

20. Barack Obama is a huge fan of Hamilton.

President Obama called the show "brilliant," adding, "so much so that I'm pretty sure this is the only thing that Dick Cheney and I have agreed on—during my entire political career."

21. Hamilton has Stephen Sondheim's seal of approval.

At some point, Miranda showed his songs to Stephen Sondheim, the man behind Into the Woods, Sweeney Todd, and many more musicals, who told The New York Times, "He sent me lyrics printed out, and recordings of the songs. This raised obvious red flags: I worried that an evening of rap might get monotonous; I thought the rhythm might become relentless. But the wonderful thing about Lin-Manuel's use of rap is that he's got one foot in the past. He knows theater ... Hamilton is a breakthrough ... We'll certainly see more rap musicals. The next thing we'll get is Lincoln set to rap. If you think I'm kidding, talk to me in a year."

22. Miranda recruited other artists for the Hamilton mixtape and a series of "Hamildrops."

In October 2015, Miranda tweeted: "So the show is done. Cast album is out. Now we begin planning The Hamilton Mixtape. Remixes & Covers & Inspired bys. FOR REAL. GET READY. I was originally trying to get the mixtape done with Atlantic before we opened, but that's like performing surgery while having a baby."

The 23-song mixtape featured artists from The Roots, Queen Latifah, and Ashanti and Ja Rule to Kelly Clarkson, Usher, and Ben Folds and Regina Spektor covering songs from the show, as well as demos of songs that didn't make the cut. There's a demo detailing the horrors the Continental Army faced at Valley Forge and a third, unreleased rap battle, "where Ham, Mad & Jeff go IN on slavery," Miranda tweeted. "It was sort of our homage to 'Hail Mary' [by Tupac Shakur]," he told Billboard.

Following the mixtape, Miranda announced a series of what he called "Hamildrops." They featured "Ben Franklin's Song" by the Decembrists, "The Hamilton Polka" by Weird Al Yankovich, an extended version of "Dear Theodosia" sung by

Sara Bareilles, and a remix of "One Last Time" featuring Barack Obama.

23. There are a few ways to interpret Eliza's gasp at the end of Hamilton.

At the end of "Who Lives, Who Dies, Who Tells Your Story," Eliza sings about her quest to ensure Hamilton's legacy: "And when my time is up, Have I done enough? Will they tell your story? Oh, I can't wait to see you again. It's only a matter of time." Alexander takes her hand, leads her around the stage, and then she steps to the edge of the stage, looks up—and gasps.

That moment isn't written into the script, and Hamilton fans have long debated what, exactly, this gasp means. Some think it's that Eliza has died and is seeing Hamilton waiting for her on the other side. Others believe that what Eliza is seeing is the audience itself—and the gasp is Eliza understanding that she succeeded in passing on his story.

"People are like, 'Is it Eliza going into heaven? Is she seeing Alexander? Is she seeing God? What is it?' And it's kind of all of those things," Soo said in a 2016 interview. "Sometimes, it's literally, I look out and I see the audience, and that's what it is, but I think that idea of 'transcendence' is present in all of that."

Miranda himself recently said that the gasp is "different for each Eliza. I've had different conversations. It's heart-stopping, isn't it? And I do think that it traverses time in some way, whether that thing she's seeing is Hamilton, whether that thing she's seeing is heaven, whether that thing she's seeing is the world now. I think those are all valid and all fair— I think she's seeing across a span of time in that moment."

One thing is for certain: Miranda is not playing himself in the final moments, leading Eliza to look out at the audience, as one fan theorized. "It's a lovely notion … but it breaks down the moment I'm not playing the role," Miranda tweeted. "The Gasp is The Gasp is The Gasp. I love all the interpretations."

B. TRIVIA QUESTION

I. "Hamilton" Trivia

Quizzes

1. The line "death doesn't discriminate/between the sinners and the saints/it takes and it takes" appears first in which song?
   A. Wait for It
   B. The World Turned Upside Down
   C. Say No to This
   D. Burn

2. Ham4Ham is a lottery system in which cast members sell front-row tickets for what amount of money?
   A. $5
   B. $10
   C. $20
   D. $100

3. Lin-Manuel Miranda started writing "Dear Theodosia" at what point in his life?
   A. When he got a dog

B. When he married his wife

C. When his child was born

D. Opening night of "In the Heights"

4. Continue the line: "I never thought I'd live past twenty."

   A. Where I come from, some get half as many.

   B. I used to go out to drink with my friend Benny.

   C. I'm lucky if I see more than one penny.

   D. We say we live fast, reach for a glass, that's plenty.

5. In the original Broadway cast, King George the Third was played by Jonathan Groff.

   A. True

   B. False

6. In the opening song, who says "I fought with him"?

   A. Madison/Hamilton

B. Jefferson/Lafayette

C. Peggy/Maria

D. George Washington

7. In the original Broadway cast, Jasmine Cephas-Jones plays which Schuyler sister?

A. Angelica

B. Peggy

C. Eliza

D. Maria

8. What is George Washington's favorite line of scripture?

A. Everyone will sit under their own vine and under their own fig tree.

B. Love is patient, love is kind.

C. For God so loved the world that he gave his one and only Son, that whoever believes in him shall not perish but have eternal life.

D. The LORD is my shepherd, I shall not be in want.

9. What compliment does Laurens get in "My Shot"?

A. I think your pants look hot

B. Let's get this guy in front of a crowd!

C. Hard rock like Lancelot

D. I like you a lot

10. There is real-life evidence that Eliza Schuyler burned the letters between herself and her husband.

A. True

B. False

11. Name the song from which these lyrics come: "Now you call me "amoral,"/ A "dangerous disgrace,"/ If you've got something to say/ Name a time and place/ Face to face"...

A. A Winter's Ball

B. Cabinet Battle #1

C. Cabinet Battle #2

D. Your Obedient Servant

12. Which ensemble member got to wear the Gypsy Robe on opening night?

A. Betsy Struxness

B. Ariana DeBose
C. Carleigh Bettiol
D. Gregory Haney

13. Which of these shows only had any of its cast or crew members participate in a Ham4Ham after the show had closed?
    A. Les Miserables
    B. RENT
    C. Fun Home
    D. Fiddler on the Roof

14. Complete the quote: "Heed not the rabble who scream 'revolution!'..."
    A. They have not your interests at heart
    B. Chaos and bloodshed are not a solution
    C. Oh my god, tear this dude apart
    D. The revolution's coming- the have-nots will win this

15. Which celebrity did NOT see "Hamilton" at some point in time?
    A. David Bowie

B. President Obama (and his family)

C. Kanye West and Kim Kardashian

D. Beyonce and Jay-Z

Answers

1. The line "death doesn't discriminate/between the sinners and the saints/it takes and it takes" appears first in which song?

   Answer: Wait for It

"Wait for It" is sung by Aaron Burr, who was played by Leslie Odom Jr in the original Broadway cast.

2. Ham4Ham is a lottery system in which cast members sell front-row tickets for what amount of money?

   Answer: $10

Not only do cast members from "Hamilton" perform at the outdoor (and sometimes online) Ham4Ham shows - cast members from nearby musicals such as "Fun Home" and "Les Mis" have also participated in raffling off Hamilton tickets!

3. Lin-Manuel Miranda started writing "Dear Theodosia" at what point in his life?
   Answer: When he got a dog

This isn't the full story - Lin says in "Hamilton: a Revolution" that they had already been struggling when they went on a vacation to the Dominican Republic with his wife's family. "My wife's aunt [...] was struggling with ALS, so the air was heavy: we dreaded/anticipated the news of her passing even as we attempted to make the best of this vacation. Amidst all this, one day a tiny stray puppy jumped up on my wife's beach chair and nipped at her ankle, with large brown eyes that pleaded, "Get me off this island." [...] Vanessa, a lifelong cat person, switched teams at that moment and Tobillo (Spanish for ankle) entered our lives for good."

4. Continue the line: "I never thought I'd live past twenty."
   Answer: Where I come from, some get half as many.

Cast member Anthony Ramos (John Laurens / Phillip Schuyler) said that he related to this quote. In the neighborhood where he grew up, it was considered lucky to live past the age of 21 because so few did.

5. In the original Broadway cast, King George the Third was played by Jonathan Groff.

Answer: True

At first, the role was given to Brian D'Arcy James. After several rehearsals, however, it was passed on to "Groffsauce", as he has been dubbed by both Mr. Miranda and the fandom.

6. In the opening song, who says "I fought with him"?

Answer: Jefferson/Lafayette

This is said together by Jefferson/Lafayette and Madison/Mulligan. Interestingly enough, the double casting is totally intentional. While Jefferson fought against Hamilton, Lafayette fought alongside him.

7. In the original Broadway cast, Jasmine Cephas-Jones plays which Schuyler sister?

Answer: Peggy

She plays Maria Reynolds (hence the "I loved him" in the opening scene alongside Angelica and Eliza).

8. What is George Washington's favorite line of scripture?

Answer: Everyone will sit under their own vine and under their own fig tree.

He apparently quoted the line often while he was alive. Lin-Manuel Miranda didn't know this until he was personally informed by Hamilton's biographer, and he decided to put the line into the musical.

9. What compliment does Laurens get in "My Shot"?
   Answer: I like you a lot

Just before this compliment to Laurens, he sang, "Mister Lafayette, hard rock like Lancelot, I think your pants look hot." The fact that Hamilton takes less than a moment to come up with personalized comments and then moves on to making revolutionary plans ("... A bunch of revolutionary manumission abolitionists?/ Give me a position, show me where the ammunition is!") is yet one more example of his rapid-fire thought.

10. There is real-life evidence that Eliza Schuyler burned the letters between herself and her husband.
    Answer: False

This is a nod to the clear lack of letters and documents. Lin tried to imagine why this was, and came up with the song "Burn", describing how Eliza went after her husband's legacy. - the thing he treasured above all else - after he made his affair with Maria Reynolds public. A Ron Chernow's biography of Hamilton asserts that she burned her letters to him, but it is that author's opinion, not a fact that was documented at the time. All we have as evidence is a lack of correspondence.

11. Name the song from which these lyrics come: "Now you call me "amoral,"/ A "dangerous disgrace,"/ If you've got something to say/ Name a time and place/ Face to face"...
     Answer: Your Obedient Servant

"Your Obedient Servant" is a shout-out to the way people back then signed their letters (the equivalent of 'sincerely'). This line is also used ironically, since "your obedient servant" implies civility while the song is an argument between Hamilton and Burr.

12. Which ensemble member got to wear the Gypsy Robe on opening night?
     Answer: Betsy Struxness

The Gypsy Robe is a theater tradition in which a chorus member with the most Broadway credits receives a robe on opening night. Before curtain, everyone associated with the show gathered onstage for the Gypsy Robe ceremony.

13. Which of these shows only had any of its cast or crew members participate in a Ham4Ham after the show had closed?
    Answer: RENT

"RENT" tells the story of a group of starving young artists struggling to survive and create a life in New York City in the thriving days of Bohemian Alphabet City during the HIV/AIDS epidemic. It ran on Broadway from 1996 to 2008, closing before "Hamilton" opened.

14. Complete the quote: "Heed not the rabble who scream 'revolution!'..."
    Answer: They have not your interests at heart

The song "Farmer Refuted" is based on an anonymously published pamphlet by Samuel Seabury signed, "A Westchester Farmer". Hamilton's responses were "A Full

Vindication of the Measures of Congress" and "The Farmer Refuted".

15. Which celebrity did NOT see "Hamilton" at some point in time?
Answer: David Bowie

Many, many famous people- from Emma Watson to Bernie Sanders have seen this show (and loved it!). The Obamas liked it so much that they invited the cast over to the White House to perform. But David Bowie never saw it before his death in 2016.

II. "Hamilton" Lyrics

Quizzes

1. In which song does Hamilton speak the following line: "You're absolutely right, John should have shot him in the mouth, that would have shut him up"?
   A. Dear Theodosia
   B. Meet Me Inside
   C. Hurricane
   D. Best of Wives and Best of Women

2. From which song does the following line come: "Don't modulate the key then not debate with me"?
   A. The Room Where It Happens
   B. Farmer Refuted
   C. What Comes Next
   D. Cabinet Battle #2

3. The fourth "Duel Commandment" details a number of things that should be done with a doctor in preparation for a duel. Which of the following is *not* mentioned?
   A. Have him turn around to have deniability
   B. Pay him in advance
   C. Double-check his utilities
   D. Treat him with civility

4. Who declares that he is "taking this horse by the reins, making redcoats redder with bloodstains"?
   A. Marquis de Lafayette
   B. Aaron Burr
   C. Alexander Hamilton
   D. Thomas Jefferson

5. In which song does King George declare, "they will tear each other into pieces, Jesus Christ this will be fun"?

   A. What Comes Next

   B. I Know Him

   C. You'll Be Back

   D. Farmer Refuted

6. Complete this line from "Satisfied", sung by Angelica: "Intelligent eyes in a hunger-pang frame, and when you said 'Hi' _____"

   A. I forgot my dang name

   B. I have never been the same

   C. It felt just like a game

   D. You set my heart aflame

7. From which song do the following lyrics come: "I'm in the cabinet, I am complicit in watching him grabbing at power and kissing it, if Washington isn't gon' listen to disciplined dissidence, this is the difference, this kid is out"?

   A. Cabinet Battle #1

   B. Washington on Your Side

C. Blow Us All Away
D. The World Was Wide Enough

8. In which song does the line, "Yo, I'm a tailor's apprentice, And I got y'all knuckleheads in loco parentis" appear?
A. My Shot
B. What'd I Miss
C. A Winter's Ball
D. Who Lives, Who Dies, Who Tells Your Story

9. Which song begins, "There are moments that the words don't reach. There is suffering too terrible to name"?
A. The Election of 1800
B. The Reynolds Pamphlet
C. Blow Us All Away

D. It's Quiet Uptown

10. As the final question, it seems appropriate to ask: What is the final line of "Hamilton"?
    A. Will they tell your story?
    B. Who tells your story?
    C. You really do write like you're running out of time
    D. Have I done enough?

11. Who was Alexander Hamilton?
    A. Treasury Secretary
    B. A General
    C. Secretary of State
    D. A Singer

12. Which of the listed characters don't re-appear onstage in Act Two?
    A. Hercules Mulligan and John Laurens
    B. John Laurens, Marquis de Lafayette and John Jay
    C. Marquis de Lafayette and James Madison
    D. John Laurens, Hercules Mulligan, and Marquis de Lafayette

13. In the title song, "Alexander Hamilton", two people say "we fought with him". Who were they?
    A. Benjamin Franklin and James Jay
    B. James Madison and John Jay
    C. Hercules Mulligan and Philip Schuyler
    D. Marquis de Lafayette and Hercules Mulligan

14. Which song in "Hamilton" has a section that is the fastest sung song on Broadway?
    A. Cabinet Battle #1
    B. Ten Duel Commandments
    C. Guns and Ships
    D. My Shot

15. Who did Alexander Hamilton have his infamous affair with?
    A. Angelica Schuyler
    B. Julia Roberts
    C. Eliza Reynolds
    D. Maria Reynolds

16. In the song "Blow Us All Away", Philip Hamilton is seeking to confront a man who publicly defamed his father, Alexander. Who was he?

A. Aaron Burr

B. John Laurens

C. John Jay

D. George Eacker

17. What is the final song in Act One?

A. Who Lives, Who Dies, Who Tells Your Story

B. Non-Stop

C. History Has Its Eyes On You

D. Blow Us All Away

18. According to Act Two of the musical, why did Aaron Burr challenge Alexander Hamilton to a duel?

A. Hamilton published lies about Burr

B. Hamilton supported Jefferson in the Election of 1800 and not Burr

C. Hamilton had an affair with Burr's wife

D. Hamilton teamed up with James Madison to keep Burr from becoming president

19. Which song does King George III NOT sing?
   A. Farmer Refuted
   B. What Comes Next
   C. You'll Be Back
   D. I Know Him

20. Who are the two characters that sing "One Last Time"?
   A. Marquis de Lafayette and Alexander Hamilton
   B. Eliza Schuyler and Alexander Hamilton
   C. Thomas Jefferson and Alexander Hamilton
   D. George Washington and Alexander Hamilton

21. Identify the song: "Let me tell you what I wish I'd known when I was young and dreamed of glory: you have no control."
   A. Alexander Hamilton
   B. My Shot
   C. One Last Time
   D. History Has Its Eyes On You

22. Identify the song: "Forgiveness, can you imagine?"
   A. It's Quiet Uptown

B. Burn

C. Take a Break

D. Say No To This

23. Identify the song: "No one really knows how the game is played, the art of the trade, how the sausage gets made."

A. The Room Where It Happens

B. Right Hand Man

C. Guns and Ships

D. Helpless

24. Identify the song: "My father's stone-faced while you're asking for his blessing. I'm dying inside as you wine and dine and I'm trying not to cry but there's nothing that your mind can't do."

A. Helpless

B. Wait For It

C. Satisfied

D. What'd I Miss

25. Identify the song: "I'm just like my country, I'm young, scrappy and hungry."
    A. Meet Me Inside
    B. Alexander Hamilton
    C. My Shot
    D. Stay Alive

26. Identify the song: "Now I'm the villain in your history."
    A. Best of Wives and Best of Women
    B. The Election of 1800
    C. Who Lives, Who Dies, Who Tells Your Story
    D. The World Was Wide Enough

27. Identify the song: "I am inimitable, I am an original."
    A. Dear Theodosia
    B. That Would Be Enough
    C. Non-Stop
    D. Wait for It

28. Identify the song: "You want a revolution? I want a revelation!"
    A. Helpless

B. The Schuyler Sisters

C. Satisfied

D. The Reynolds Pamphlet

29. Identify the song: "Life, liberty and the pursuit of happiness. We fought for these ideals; we shouldn't settle for less. These are wise words, enterprising men quote em, don't act surprised, you guys, 'cause I wrote em!"

A. Cabinet Battle #1

B. What'd I Miss

C. Cabinet Battle #2

D. The Adams Administration

30. Identify the song: "You have married an Icarus. He has flown too close to the sun".

A. Blow Us All Away

B. Helpless

C. Burn

D. Hurricane

Answers

1. In which song does Hamilton speak the following line: "You're absolutely right, John should have shot him in the mouth, that would have shut him up"?
    Answer: Meet Me Inside

In "Meet Me Inside" George Washington orders Alexander Hamilton to return home from the war. John Laurens shot Charles Lee in the waist during their duel, and in this line Hamilton demonstrates his lack of remorse for permitting the duel to occur.

2. From which song does the following line come: "Don't modulate the key then not debate with me"?
    Answer: Farmer Refuted

In this song, Samuel Seabury argues against the revolution. Hamilton interjects and attempts to debate with him. This is one of multiple instances in "Hamilton" where the characters show awareness of the music: the score does, indeed, modulate up a half-step just prior to this line.

3. The fourth "Duel Commandment" details a number of things that should be done with a doctor in preparation for a duel. Which of the following is *not* mentioned?

Answer: Double-check his utilities

The "Ten Duel Commandments" recur throughout the musical. In total, there are three duels: Laurens vs Lee; Phillip Hamilton vs George Eacker; and, of course, Alexander Hamilton vs Aaron Burr. Having the doctor "turn around to have deniability" is a means of protecting the doctor - if his back is turned, he can honestly say he didn't witness anything. Paying him in advance and treating him with civility are sensible if you want the doctor to do his best to treat you if necessary.

4. Who declares that he is "taking this horse by the reins, making redcoats redder with bloodstains"?
   Answer: Marquis de Lafayette

This line comes from "Guns and Ships", a song that requires Lafayette to rap at breakneck speed. Lafayette convinces Washington that, if they are to win at Yorktown, Hamilton must take the lead. In the original Broadway production, Daveed Diggs played Lafayette in Act 1 and Jefferson in Act 2. He won the Tony for Best Supporting Actor in a Musical.

5. In which song does King George declare, "they will tear each other into pieces, Jesus Christ this will be fun"?
    Answer: I Know Him

King George appears on stage for a mere nine minutes, yet manages to squeeze in three songs. In "I Know Him", King George discovers that John Adams is to be the new President of the United States. King George is very critical of the Americans seeking independence and believes they would be better off under his rule.

6. Complete this line from "Satisfied", sung by Angelica: "Intelligent eyes in a hunger-pang frame, and when you said 'Hi' _____ "
    Answer: I forgot my dang name

In the previous song, "Helpless", we see Alexander and Eliza meet for the first time. In "Satisfied", we rewind back in time (the characters move backwards and the turntable in the floor spins in the opposite direction) and view the scene from Angelica's point of view. This ties into the musical's overall theme that everybody will have a different version of history and how things happened. "I forgot my dang name" refers, on the surface, to the euphoric feeling of attraction, but it also reflects Angelica momentarily forgetting that she is a

Schuyler and has familial responsibilities to marry rich, as she realises later in the song. In real life, however, Angelica was not the eldest Schuyler child and, indeed, was already married when she met Alexander.

7. From which song do the following lyrics come: "I'm in the cabinet, I am complicit in watching him grabbing at power and kiss it, if Washington isn't gon' listen to disciplined dissidence, this is the difference, this kid is out"?
   Answer: Washington on Your Side

It is during this moment that Thomas Jefferson realises that he must resign from the Cabinet. This passage uses a dactylic meter (a stressed syllable followed by two unstressed syllables) along with internal false rhyme, assonance and alliteration. Dactyls, a relatively uncommon meter, are also used in Lafayette's blistering rap: "No one has more resilience or matches my practical tactical brilliance". This serves as a reference to the fact that Lafayette and Jefferson is a dual role, played by one actor.

8. In which song does line, "Yo, I'm a tailor's apprentice, And I got y'all knuckleheads in loco parentis" appear?
   Answer: My Shot

This is how Hercules Mulligan introduces himself. "Loco parentis" is Latin for "in the place of parents". This has a double-meaning in the show: he is saying that he views his friends as parental figures, but it also refers to the notion of Founding Fathers.

9. Which song begins, "There are moments that the words don't reach. There is suffering too terrible to name"?

Answer: It's Quiet Uptown

This heartbreaking song details the grief of Alexander and Eliza following the death of their son, Phillip. Together, they slowly begin to piece their lives back together as Eliza forgives Alexander for his adultery. The following song begins with Jefferson asking "Can we get back to politics?", which offers the audience a reprieve from the confronting emotions of "It's Quiet Uptown".

10. As the final question, it seems appropriate to ask: What is the final line of "Hamilton"?

Answer: Who tells your story?

All of these lines come from the show's final song, "Who Lives, Who Dies, Who Tells Your Story". The show ends with the cast directly asking the audience who tells their stories.

This musical ends in an emotional, tender way. While there are harmonies and orchestrations throughout the song, the final word is sung a cappella and as a single, unified note.

11. Who was Alexander Hamilton?
    Answer: Treasury Secretary

He was the very first Secretary of the Treasury, to be exact. He acted as George Washington's right hand man during the American Revolution, and after the war he was promoted to create a national bank.

12. Which of the listed characters don't re-appear onstage in Act Two?
    Answer: John Laurens, Hercules Mulligan, and Marquis de Lafayette

John Laurens dies in battle during the Revolution, Marquis de Lafayette went back to France after the Revolution, and Mulligan just was written out of the play after that point because he didn't do much after the Revolution.

13. In the title song, "Alexander Hamilton", two people say "we fought with him". Who were they?

Answer: Marquis de Lafayette and Hercules Mulligan

Lin Manuel Miranda was very sneaky with this line because in Act One, Lafayette and Mulligan physically fight with Hamilton in the revolution, but the actors who play them in the original production also play Jefferson and Madison in Act Two, who also verbally fought with Hamilton.

14. Which song in "Hamilton" has a section that is the fastest sung song on Broadway?
    Answer: Guns and Ships

Lafayette spits out 19 words in 3 seconds (6.333 words per second) in this song in Act One. The song previously holding that fastest song title was "Not Getting Married Today" from the musical "Company", which had 6.2 words per second.

15. Who did Alexander Hamilton have his infamous affair with?
    Answer: Maria Reynolds

He cheated on his wife, Eliza, and was blackmailed by James Reynolds (Maria's husband) and Hamilton paid him off. He was caught sending Mr. Reynolds money and was accused of sending government funds (because he was Secretary of the

Treasury, so he had access to government funds) and he was forced to publicly publish and admit his affair.

16. In the song "Blow Us All Away", Philip Hamilton is seeking to confront a man who publicly defamed his father, Alexander. Who was he?
Answer: George Eacker

Philip called Mr. Eacker out on publicly defaming his father and challenged him to a duel that took place in New Jersey. Philip was shot by Mr. Eacker and later died.

17. What is the final song in Act One?
Answer: Non-Stop

"Non-Stop" ends the First Act. The song begins with Hamilton completing a degree at King's College, and he and Burr, become lawyers in New York. Hamilton uses his skills with a quill and his knowledge from being a lawyer to defend the United States Constitution. He wrote the Federalist Papers with James Madison and John Jay and, as the title states, he was "Non-Stop". Hamilton wrote a total of 51 essays defending the document in 6 months.

18. According to Act Two of the musical, why did Aaron Burr challenge Alexander Hamilton to a duel?
Answer: Hamilton supported Jefferson in the Election of 1800 and not Burr

Hamilton showed his support for Jefferson, despite being closer with Burr. Burr saw this act as the reason he lost the election, and challenged Hamilton to a duel through letters that were sent back and forth between the two. This can be heard in the song "Your Obedient Servant" in Act Two.

19. Which song does King George III NOT sing?
Answer: Farmer Refuted

He sings two songs in Act One, "You'll Be Back" and "What Comes Next?" and one song in Act Two, "I Know Him". "Farmer Refuted" is sung by his loyal defender, Samuel Seabury, in Act One, delivering notice that the King doesn't approve of the Revolution.

20. Who are the two characters that sing "One Last Time"?
Answer: George Washington and Alexander Hamilton

This is the song that George Washington sings when he tells Hamilton that he is stepping down from his position as president.

In the song, both Hamilton and Washington recite George Washington's actual farewell address word for word during this song.

21. Identify the song: "Let me tell you what I wish I'd known when I was young and dreamed of glory: you have no control."
    Answer: History Has Its Eyes On You

Song is sung by George Washington in Act One when he is telling Hamilton that he needs to take a step back because when he was young he was given a lot of power and didn't know how to use it. He's letting Hamilton know to be careful.

22. Identify the song: "Forgiveness, can you imagine?"
    Answer: It's Quiet Uptown

This song is sung after Alexander Hamilton and Eliza lose Philip in Act Two, and they have to learn to deal with their misfortunes.

23. Identify the song: "No one really knows how the game is played, the art of the trade, how the sausage gets made."

Answer: The Room Where It Happens

This song is sung by Aaron Burr in Act Two when Thomas Jefferson, James Maddison and Hamilton have a private meeting to discuss trades and government issues. They don't invite Burr, and Burr wants to be in "the room where it happens".

24. Identify the song: "My father's stone-faced while you're asking for his blessing. I'm dying inside as you wine and dine and I'm trying not to cry but there's nothing that your mind can't do."

Answer: Helpless

Eliza is singing this song in Act One after she meets Hamilton for the first time; they wed two weeks later.

25. Identify the song: "I'm just like my country, I'm young, scrappy and hungry."

Answer: My Shot

Hamilton sings this song in Act One as he arrives in New York and meets his friends Laurens, Mulligan and Lafayette. He sings about how he is going to rise to the top and not let anything get in his way.

26. Identify the song: "Now I'm the villain in your history."
    Answer: The World Was Wide Enough

Burr sings this song at the end of Act Two after he shoots Hamilton and realizes that Hamilton wasn't really a threat. They could have both lived peacefully together because the world was wide enough for both of them.

27. Identify the song: "I am inimitable, I am an original."
    Answer: Wait for It

Burr sings this song in Act One after he tells his friends that he's been seeing a married woman and that he would do anything to keep her because "love doesn't discriminate between the sinners and the saints". He goes into detail about his family and the death of his parents and his life and how everything is unfair to everyone.

28. Identify the song: "You want a revolution? I want a revelation!"

Answer: The Schuyler Sisters

Angelica Schuyler sings this song in Act One with her sisters. It is just a fun loving song about how they want change and how they're keeping their eyes open for a mind at work.

29. Identify the song: "Life, liberty and the pursuit of happiness. We fought for these ideals; we shouldn't settle for less. These are wise words, enterprising men quote em, don't act surprised, you guys, 'cause I wrote em!"

Answer: Cabinet Battle #1

Thomas Jefferson sings that line in Act Two when Hamilton tries to establish a national bank. That included the government assuming state debts, which Jefferson wasn't too fond of.

30. Identify the song: "You have married an Icarus. He has flown too close to the sun".

Answer: Burn

Eliza sings this in Act Two when she finds out that Hamilton has been having an affair behind her back. These are the words she actually quotes from Angelica, her sister.

III. Photo Quizzes

1. Lin-Manuel Miranda may have won several awards for writing and starring in "Hamilton", but the 2016 Tony Award for Best Actor in a Musical went to his co-star, Leslie Odom, Jr. Which character did Odom, Jr., play, who was "the villain in [Hamilton's] history"?

   A. Thomas Jefferson
   B. James Madison
   C. Aaron Burr
   D. John Laurens

2. The 2016 Tony Award for Best Featured Actor in a Musical went to Daveed Diggs, who plays a double role in the show. Diggs played Marquis de Lafayette in Act I, but which Francophile president did he play in Act II?

A. James Monroe
B. John Adams
C. James Madison
D. Thomas Jefferson

3. Three Schuyler sisters make an appearance in the musical. Which of these is NOT one of the Schuyler sisters?

A. Peggy
B. Angelica
C. Maria
D. Eliza

4. According to Aaron Burr, who "named her feral tomcat after" Alexander Hamilton?

A. Betsy Ross
B. Martha Washington
C. Abigail Adams
D. Lucy Knox

5. In his letters to Angelica, Alexander Hamilton quotes and references a "Scottish tragedy". To which Shakespearean play is Hamilton referring?

A. Hamlet
B. Othello
C. King Lear
D. Macbeth

6. In "The Room Where it Happens", Burr tells Hamilton that Clermont Street was renamed after this Revolutionary War general who died. Whose legacy was secured when they renamed the street?

A. Schuyler
B. Mercer
C. Henry
D. Washington

7. Who wrote "The Reynolds Pamphlet", detailing Alexander Hamilton's affair with Mrs. Reynolds?

A. Aaron Burr
B. John Laurens
C. James Reynolds
D. Alexander Hamilton

8. Who fatally shoots Alexander Hamilton's son Philip in a duel?

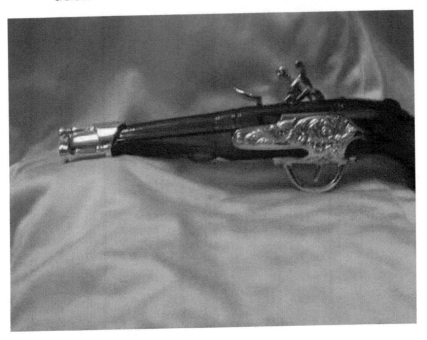

A. Aaron Burr
B. Charles Lee
C. George Eacker
D. Samuel Seabury

9. Alexander Hamilton died from injuries he received during a duel with Aaron Burr. Burr shot Hamilton in the ribs. Where did Hamilton shoot Burr?

A. he didn't - he shot in the air
B. the arm
C. the leg
D. the ear

10. After Alexander Hamilton's death, his wife Eliza went on to co-found the first of these in New York City. What is it?

A. private orphanage
B. taxi and limousine company
C. correspondence school
D. suffrage society

11. Which historian wrote the 2004 biography "Hamilton" that inspired the creation of "Hamilton: An American Musical"? (Look at the sphere in the picture and consider other words to describe it to lead you to the correct answer.)

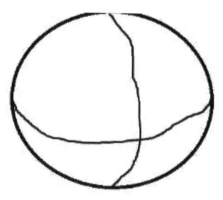

A. Ron Chernow
B. Stephen Ambrose
C. David McCullough
D. Peter Petre

12. Lin-Manuel Miranda is certainly a name that has come up in connection with "Hamilton". Which role did he play in both the off-Broadway production and the original Broadway cast? (Consider the place that is shown in this stamp--if you look closely, you can see its name--and who might have a connection with it.)

A. Alexander Hamilton
B. Thomas Jefferson
C. George Washington
D. Aaron Burr

13. In the musical, Hamilton was a resident of which state? (Look at the stamp and you see an image of a bridge at the border of Ontario and this state.)

A. Massachusetts
B. South Carolina
C. Virginia
D. New York

14. Ambitious to rise in the world, Hamilton married one of the daughters of the wealthy Schuyler family. Which one? (Who do you see in this stamp?--A bit of translation might help.)

A. Angelica
B. Peggy
C. Cornelia
D. Eliza

15. One of the best places to read Hamilton's thoughts on government--especially the US Federal Government--is in "The Federalist Papers". He worked with two other collaborators. Which man did not work with him on this project? (As a hint, consider what is clearly marked on this man, what this is called, and look at the four answers.)

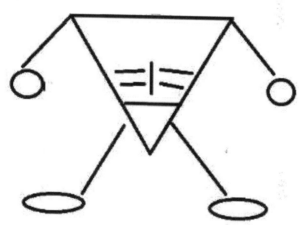

A. Aaron Burr
B. John Jay
C. James Madison
D. All three worked with him

16. In the musical (and in real life) who succeeded Washington as the second president of the United States? (Look at what is on the stamp and think about which part of the US that object is associated with.)

A. James Madison
B. Alexander Hamilton
C. John Adams
D. Thomas Jefferson

17. The Election of 1800 dragged on and on as there was no clear victor as referenced in the song "The Election of 1800". When the election went to the House of Representatives, which candidate did Hamilton throw his support behind? (Consider the person that would be associated with the location shown on the stamp.)

A. Thomas Jefferson
B. John Adams
C. Aaron Burr
D. John Laurens

18. In the musical, how did Hamilton die? (Look at the stamp.)

A. He drowns
B. He is stabbed
C. He dies of old age
D. He is shot

Answers

1. Lin-Manuel Miranda may have won several awards for writing and starring in "Hamilton", but the 2016 Tony Award for Best Actor in a Musical went to his co-star, Leslie Odom, Jr. Which character did Odom, Jr., play, who was "the villain in [Hamilton's] history"?
   Answer: Aaron Burr

"Hamilton" was nominated for 16 Tony Awards, but it had multiple nominations in the Best Actor in a Musical and Best Featured Actor in a Musical. The show won 11 Tonys, including Best Musical. The only category where the show was nominated but did not win was "Best Scenic Design of a Musical", which went to "She Loves Me".

2. The 2016 Tony Award for Best Featured Actor in a Musical went to Daveed Diggs, who plays a double role in the show. Diggs played Marquis de Lafayette in Act I, but which Francophile president did he play in Act II?
   Answer: Thomas Jefferson

There are several double roles in the play, with an actor playing one role in Act I and another role in Act II. These roles are not just a matter of convenience, as they are foreshadowed in the opening song.

Both Hercules Mulligan and Marquis de Lafayette sing "we fought with him", and those characters do fight alongside Hamilton in Act I. But those roles are shared with James Madison and Thomas Jefferson, respectively, and those characters fight with Hamilton politically in Act II.

John Laurens sings "I died for him", and Laurens dies during the war in Act I. (The scene where Hamilton receives a letter from Laurens' father telling him so is not on the cast album). That role is shared with Philip, Hamilton's son who dies in a duel in Act II.

When all three Schuyler sisters sing "I loved him", it's easy to see why Angelica and Eliza have the line. But Peggy also sings it, which references her role as Maria Reynolds in Act II.

3. Three Schuyler sisters make an appearance in the musical. Which of these is NOT one of the Schuyler sisters?
    Answer: Maria

Despite Angelica singing that her "father has no sons", that's just not true. He had several sons, including Philip Jeremiah Schuyler who went on to serve in the US House of Representatives. However, this inaccuracy helps define the character of Angelica in the musical as a "modern" intellectual woman.

Another inaccuracy? That Angelica was a serious rival for Alexander Hamilton's wooing of Eliza. Angelica had eloped with John Church in 1777, and Hamilton met the Schuylers in 1780.

Alexander Hamilton had an affair with Maria Reynolds.

Oh, and Peggy's first name was actually Margarita.

4. According to Aaron Burr, who "named her feral tomcat after" Alexander Hamilton?
    Answer: Martha Washington

Despite Hamilton agreeing to this fact ("That's true.") in the next line of the musical, this is a false story, most likely spread by John Adams later in Hamilton's career.

Ron Chernow, the author of the biography that the musical is based upon, served as a producer and historical fact checker on the musical. This isn't to say that the musical is completely accurate, just that the inaccuracies helped tell the story.

5. In his letters to Angelica, Alexander Hamilton quotes and references a "Scottish tragedy". To which Shakespearean play is Hamilton referring?
    Answer: Macbeth

Despite Hamilton claiming that Angelica will "understand the reference to another Scottish tragedy without my having to name the play", the next line is "they think of me as Macbeth".

Angelica references Macbeth later in the scene when she tells Hamilton to "screw your courage to the sticking place".

The inclusion of Macbeth is noteworthy because, traditionally, theater performers are superstitious of Macbeth and try to avoid even mentioning the name, which may be why Hamilton tries to avoid stating it in his letter.

6. In "The Room Where it Happens", Burr tells Hamilton that Clermont Street was renamed after this Revolutionary War general who died. Whose legacy was secured when they renamed the street?
   Answer: Mercer

The inclusion of this fact about General Mercer was a result of trying to rhyme "Burr, sir". Lin-Manuel Miranda was able to link a general who died during the Revolutionary War to Mercer Street in the Village, which worked wonderfully in a song about legacy.

7. Who wrote "The Reynolds Pamphlet", detailing Alexander Hamilton's affair with Mrs. Reynolds?
   Answer: Alexander Hamilton

The truth is a little more complicated than it is presented in the musical. After being confronted by James Monroe, Alexander Hamilton explained the situation and expected the matter to remain private. However, details came to light in a series of writings by James Callender published in 1797.

This prompted Hamilton to respond by writing "Observations on Certain Documents Contained" in No. V & VI of "The History of the United States for the Year 1796, In which the Charge of Speculation Against Alexander Hamilton, Late Secretary of the Treasury, is Fully Refuted", more commonly known as "The Reynolds Pamphlet". In this pamphlet, Hamilton defends himself against the accusations of embezzlement but admits to the affair and blackmail, which, as evidenced in the musical, had a terrible price.

8. Who fatally shoots Alexander Hamilton's son Philip in a duel?
    Answer: George Eacker

In 1801, George Eacker (who was a supporter of Aaron Burr) made a speech insulting Alexander Hamilton. Philip confronted Eacker about it on November 21, and the next day they had their first duel.

That's right, the first duel ended without injuries, so the two went at it again the next day. The shot that killed 19-year old Philip Hamilton happened during the second duel.

When Philip first challenged Eacker, Eacker was watching a play. That play was "The West Indian". Alexander Hamilton was born in the West Indies, which is an odd coincidence.

9. Alexander Hamilton died from injuries he received during a duel with Aaron Burr. Burr shot Hamilton in the ribs. Where did Hamilton shoot Burr?
   Answer: he didn't - he shot in the air

Shooting in the air as part of a duel was a way of ending the conflict honorably while avoiding injury. The technical term is "delope", which is French for "throwing away". So at the end, Hamilton literally did "[throw] away [his] shot".

One nod to historical accuracy is that Hamilton wore his glasses during the duel, which means that Hamilton has to wear glasses at some points earlier in the musical to set that up.

10. After Alexander Hamilton's death, his wife Eliza went on to co-found the first of these in New York City. What is it?

Answer: private orphanage

Eliza co-founded the Orphan Asylum Society in 1806, and was named second directress (vice-president). In 1821, she began a 27-year run as first directress, leading the organization in that role until she left in 1848 to live with her daughter in Washington, D.C.

Since 1977, the organization has been known as Graham Windham as a result of several mergers. It still continues to provide social services for children.

11. Which historian wrote the 2004 biography "Hamilton" that inspired the creation of "Hamilton: An American Musical"?

Answer: Ron Chernow

If you think of a sphere as "round", you might have guessed the correct answer was "Ron" Chernow (a similar clue). Born in 1949, Ron Chernow has written several other biographies including ones about John D. Rockefeller and George Washington (for which he won the Pulitzer Prize). His biography about Alexander Hamilton spent three months on the New York Times bestseller list. Ron Chernow served as a historical consultant for the production of the musical.

12. Lin-Manuel Miranda is certainly a name that has come up in connection with "Hamilton". Which role did he play in both the off-Broadway production and the original Broadway cast?
    Answer: Alexander Hamilton

Born in 1980, Lin-Manuel Miranda is a native New Yorker of Puerto Rican descent. In addition to playing the title role, Miranda also wrote the book, lyrics, and music for the show. Best known for "Hamilton", Miranda also wrote the 2012 musical "Bring It On". The place in the stamp is Columbia University, which Hamilton attended. Burr attended Princeton, Jefferson attended William and Mary, and Washington did not attend college.

13. In the musical, Hamilton was a resident of which state?
    Answer: New York

Hamilton moved from the West Indies to New York City as a teenager to attend King's College (now Columbia University). In real life, as in the musical, Hamilton was part of an artillery company that participated in the defense of New York City in 1776. Hamilton later signed the Constitution as a delegate from New York. The Niagara Falls Bridge spans from Ontario to New York

14. Ambitious to rise in the world, Hamilton married one of the daughters of the wealthy Schuyler family. Which one?

Answer: Eliza

The stamp shows Queen Isabella of Spain. Isabella is Spanish for Elizabeth. Elizabeth Schuyler was usually referred to as Eliza in the musical. Elizabeth Schuyler (1757-1854) lived to be almost 100 and outlived Hamilton by 50 years. Elizabeth and Hamilton had eight children together. After his death, she was heavily involved in preserving his legacy and also in various charitable works. The relationship of Eliza and Hamilton is a major theme of the musical.

15. One of the best places to read Hamilton's thoughts on government--especially the US Federal Government--is in "The Federalist Papers". He worked with two other collaborators. Which man did not work with him on this project?

Answer: Aaron Burr

The initial purpose of "The Federalist Papers" was to convince the voters of New York State to ratify the US Constitution. Alexander Hamilton was the most active member of the three, writing more than half of the 85 essays in the collection. James Madison (1751-1836) was also active, writing a significant number including the famous Number 10 which describes how the Constitution will weaken the spirit of faction. John Jay (1745-1825) only wrote five of the essays, but can be excused as he suffered from a sickness during much of the period (1787-1788) when the essays were written. In the musical, Hamilton approaches Burr to join the collaboration, but Burr turns him down. Aaron Burr (1756-1836) in real-life was an important anti-Federalist in New York. In the drawing, I hoped that you would notice that the man's stomach muscles or "abs" were emphasized and that "ab" would get you to "A" aron "B" urr.

16. In the musical (and in real life) who succeeded Washington as the second president of the United States?
Answer: John Adams

In real life, Jefferson was the third president and Madison was the fourth. Hamilton himself never served as President and as much the musical might show us Hamilton's good side, I think Hamilton would have been hard pressed to have won enough votes even from the restricted electorate of the late 1700s and early 1800s. The song "The Adams Administration" reflects the real-life coolness of relations between Hamilton and Adams. The stamp shows the "Mayflower" which landed at Plymouth which is now part of Massachusetts (home state of John Adams.)

17. The Election of 1800 dragged on and on as there was no clear victor as referenced in the song "The Election of 1800". When the election went to the House of Representatives, which candidate did Hamilton throw his support behind?

    Answer: Thomas Jefferson

As originally established by the Constitution, each state had a number of electors based on the number of representatives and senators sent to Congress. Each elector was chosen in a manner of the state's choosing (popular vote, appointment by the state legislature, etc.). Each elector voted for two choices (presumably one was for president and one for vice president). The candidate with the most votes would be president and the candidate with the second most votes would be vice president. In 1796, the president (John Adams) and vice president (Thomas Jefferson) belonged to different parties. In 1800, two candidates from the same party (Jefferson and Aaron Burr) received the same number of votes and more than any other candidate. The election then went to the House of Representatives where each state's delegation had one vote. Hamilton felt that Jefferson was a better choice than Burr to be president and was able to convince enough representatives to change their votes or not vote to allow Jefferson to win. The stamp shows the Louisiana Purchase which occurred during Jefferson's presidency.

18. In the musical, how did Hamilton die? (Look at the stamp.)

    Answer: He is shot

In Weehawken, NJ, in 1804, Hamilton and Burr fought their famous duel. Hamilton purposely shot his pistol into the air while Burr's shot wounded Hamilton fatally. There is irony to Hamilton's often repeated line "I am not throwing away my shot." Yet, Hamilton is far more positively remembered today than Burr is.

Made in United States
Orlando, FL
27 October 2022